THE DREAMER

Poems of Fubbi

MODESTE HERLIC

Author's edition
2nd Edition
2022

THE
DREAMER
Poems of Fubbi

Translated by Modeste Herlic

To Sarah
for her friendship

CONTENTS

Courage

Live the present moment
for the days are uncertain
and your life will not last forever
Be yourself today and now
and do what makes you happy

8

Be not burdened by the glares of others
Your back is so soft, so delicate
Be strong
Hold your head high
and ignore the envious

Every night
I go to my window
and plant seeds
of smiles in the bowl
I have a great love
for the nightingale
Every morning
o sweet bird!
Every morning
your song is bliss
your whistle is poetry

Fortune knocks at your door
and you refuse to open it
That is nonsense!
It is stupidity on your part
when you do not accept
that life is beautiful
and that everything is possible

Yesterday I dreamed
that I was the wind
filling the world
Everywhere I went
At every party I danced
In every corner I slept
I saw men crying
I saw men partying
I walked by them
and danced with them
in the downfall and the merriment

With my golden lute
I sang to the world:
"o-o-o-o-o-o-o-o-om
o-o-o-o-o-o-o-o-o-om
how wonderful it is to hear the universe
how infinite is this rejoicing"

The saddest ones forgot their sorrow
They danced and hummed
My melody became their feast
Roses grew in their gardens
And we all sang:
"o-o-o-o-o-o-o-o-om
o-o-o-o-o-o-o-o-o-om
how wonderful it is to hear the universe
how infinite is this rejoicing"

12

I took the bow of victory
Tiger, wolf, and panther
walk in my shadow
I am the lion who falls
and rises again

13

What dwells at the end of sorrow?
Do you know?
What I know is
at the end of every night
the sun always opens a smile

You who are breathless
under the weight of despair
let go of bitterness
let go of fear
Breathe
deep to the ends of rest
deep to the land of the Soul
Open your heart
feel the arrival of Joy
let It enter
your innermost being
and be filled with bliss

Why are you depressed
and plagued by yesterday's failure?
Observe Life around you
In the garden of new beginnings
the flowers radiate the fragrance of Love
the green willow shines
In the surroundings
the laws of nature rule
amidst the eternal Beauty

The landscape, a green and reddish scene
of which you are the unique painter
If you feel your heart
look at the horizon
trust in the sunrise
and listen carefully
For every crow of the cock
heralds a new journey
Why lament today
if tomorrow is a new day?

From now on, all I want to do
is carry a basket full of smiles
as I wander back and forth
like a rain cloud
over the world and its mysteries
If I should fall
I will fall light
I will fall softly
sweet as the drops of contentment

O shining Sun!
The eye that sees all
the star that knows all
Listen to my song
for I sing your name

On the road of Life
time never stops
but in the deep sea of heaven
my poem turns and turns
with no end
no beginning

I smile, not because my life is perfect
I smile because with a light heart
the burden of Life weighs less than a feather
And with this, I write lines of Love
for you to remember
that your life is beautiful

Life was made for you
It is all for you
and without you in it
there is no me
So when you feel exhausted
remember:
"All the beauty in the world
all the charm of the universe
all this is for you
it is for you to enjoy
it is for you to live"

When life robs me of happiness
I go to the ruins of my heart
take the least broken bricks
and build the tower of hope

Since self-will escapes me
I go searching for the will of heaven
It is there
in the middle of the night
in the heavenly garden
where flowers are wine
where joy is a molten meadow
I will lie there, serene
O heaven's will!
Let your golden rays
and your jewels
fall upon me

22

One day
I heard a wise man say:
"Love erases badly written lines."
Vain or deceitful phrases
all beauty fades
before Love
like a wicked flower
in the springtime bower

23

In the notebook of Life
only Love corrects mistakes
In the notebook of Life
only Love writes again
And Love always writes
with the best ink

24

You touch the moon in your daydream
because nothing, under the sun,
can limit your dreams

25

Believe in yourself
and have the courage to say
"I love you"
to that person
before it is too late

26

The man that I am
will not let the search for bread
adorn the hunger of the Soul
The man that I am
will not let the taste of wine
hides the thirst of the Soul

There is a secret hidden
in the heart of the rose
that I gave to my beloved
It is the same secret
in my core
Is this the Answer of answers?
The riddle that would quench the hunger
and the thirst of the Soul?

I stop everything and leave
the trivialities of this world
far from this life
populated by fools
full of passions
I will walk
surrendered to the softness of the breeze
with a serene motion and a liberated spirit

At every step forward
you seem to crumble
Hope is saddened
Weariness burns your faith
But before you give up
lift your vision
and remember:
*"At the end of each night
the dawn is waiting
for a new day to come
a new chance
to be true to yourself"*

Deep inside
I am a breath of wind
fresh and eternal
created to make air
in the existence
where days are roses
where nights are fragrances

Under the yoke of day
the glorious sun
awakens my vision
In the heart of night
the bright moon
illuminates my mission
The journey seems eternal
but the way is clear
and the shining stars
in the endless sky
chant the song of Love
The melodies of the universe
surround me

32

How can Life hurt me?
I am not even born
eternal as time
I am a Soul
that does not bleed
neither color nor face
neither mind nor body
I am
a mystery to myself

Life is not a place to perish
and if it is
I do not want to know
I will let Death take its course
I want to open the drawer
and change my clothes
There are a thousand lives
waiting for me
in the dining room

Death, Death?
What do you mean?
I am a river
My dance never ends
My wanderings are eternal
My song is permanent
I cross the world
but remain the same
always wandering
always resting

Have love in your eyes
in your gestures
in your speeches
in your thoughts
in your dreams
Have love
and say no more
Have love
though life seems to mock you
and people seem to oppress you
Have love
and ask nothing in return
Because to have *"love"*
is to have everything

When you reach the stars
you will look down the mountain
breathe in the pure air of victory
It will all have been worth it

For a thousand lifetimes
I suffered without ceasing
So I wanted to meet
the merciful Soul
and when I gave myself to It
I found Myself
Neither time nor space defined Me
My compassion had no place on earth
I am the vastness
bigger than the world that holds me

38

No fear can conquer
my inner love
and deep inside
I am a king
of a great kingdom

People say
that you speak through riddles
that your poem is not poetry
that you do not follow the rules
that your mind escapes logic
that your words are disturbing
They say many things
But when I look at you
only silence echoes

Waves of wealth come and go
Waves of sorrow come and go
But I am the infinite sea
All rivers serve me
What shall I fear?

I am a human being
I have many imperfections
and many qualities
I lack many virtues
but some principles make me great
Among these
I am proud of only one
which I always carry with me:
"love"

42

I learned to love life
though it oppresses me
though I am not worthy
of its forgiveness
I love life
and love
is the only virtue
that does not condemn me

In the azure firmament
there are infinite rays of gold
that come down like a rainstorm
Today I intend to go out
like a madman
I want to run for joy
throw myself on the warm sand
I wish only one thing
for all the sky to fall on me!

Before the mountain
that touches the sky
the discouraged disciple
bowed his head
Then the master said:
"The true victor
cares not for the future,
not for the past.
He knows no fear.
Like the wind of life,
he goes forward,
without regret,
always true to his dreams
and aspirations"

45

Wherever I go, I will conquer the world
I keep the sunrise in my words
There is no darkness for me
I was born to overcome negativity
and I will win all wars

46

My heart is always true
outward, or inward
No foe can withstand my kindness

When the night comes
stars become flowers
in the deep sea of the sky

Angels celebrate far away from the mind
while people dance around the fire

I lie down
wrap myself in a blanket
lonely in my little nest
Here I am all alone
far from my countrymen
With a lightness on my lips
I sleep peacefully
and dream of angels
celebrating in Nirvana

Who said that the night is terrifying?
From where I stand, I see only diamonds
In the dark blue, they all glitter in the moonlight
All this brightness comes from the sleeping sun
No one can escape the golden glow
not even the moon, who has gray eyes
The night is not frightening
It is bright and a good counselor
for those who have clarity of mind

O Supreme
how I love You
in the simplicity of life
in the beauty of the universe

When the breeze
touches my face
I feel Your sweet caress

In the blue sky
neither clear nor dark
the golden and stormy clouds
form the Unity

O Supreme
Your gentle Face
a delight to the Soul
I trust in You
"Eternal Love"
Guide my path
through this new cycle

I am the universe

51

The flowers of the landscape
are more than green
In the surroundings
they are jewels of gold

52

The universe speaks in words
that have no sound
but the man whose heart is kind
can hear the songs of the wind

The journey is long
My mission is unknown
But above me, lies the endless blue
a dark blue sea of glittering stars
I gently lift my eyes
Wonderful, wonderful!
There is nothing more beautiful

54

The answers of the world
gathered in one breath
Now that I know the truth
I lay down
serene and full of grace

55

The things that we have done
the things that we will do
are all atoms of the wind
that roll across the river
The steps of the whirlwind
go back to the beginning
to the origin of the universes

By the river
the breeze dances
and its movement
astonishes the branches
of trees and leaves
The air whispers notes and chords
that move the surface of the water
What a rhythm!
What a delight, that singing melody!
Dance, divine wind
Sing, divine breeze
Life is a song
Life is a dance

Listen to my voice
I am the wind
Listen to my song:

"The panther runs and tires
The tortoise walks and rests
The panther leaps with eagerness
The tortoise lies down quietly
The panther searches for the target
The tortoise follows the path"

Rest, my friend
Please, rest
Have faith
and trust in my song
The path is me
I am the wind of overcoming

58

In every night of mine
oceans of dreams stretch out
They are stories of many worlds
hidden in tidal waves
Waves that transcend time
It is no conceit to think
that I am eternal

Songs of Joy

Come on, my fellow men
Come along, everybody
Let yourselves go
Shake off the longing
Set the joy free
Listen to the heart
that wants to bloom
stretched out like a star
majestic as water lily
if you move
if you allow yourself
to sing with birds
to dance with butterflies

Life is an uncertain journey
a journey with a thousand destinations
a navigation over a thousand seas
seas of a thousand waves
waves of a thousand dances

I hope one day
mankind will be a dancer
and all its troubles
will become waltz steps

At the window
the stream of joy
"Merrily, merrily"
O friendly bird!
There is no better way
to start my day

O life
pleasant mirth
the bliss of dancing
the pleasure of singing
It is all worth it
And if I must live again
I will do it with more joy

Drops of water rejoice on the sea
Birds of Joy sing in the sky
Life is a shooting star
Do not miss its show
Watch it, before it is too late
You cannot see it
because you spend the day in longing
Too much longing means boredom
Let go of the past
The *"Merry Boat"*
only goes by once

The heart of the perfect sailor
goes blind and loves everybody
It is now or never
Jump on the *"Merry Boat"*
See the dancing water
and the flying fish
The dawn is shining on us
with golden teeth
O how wonderful is the *"Merry boat"*!

Sing and dance
now and forever
The stars want to hear
They aim to stir
They wish to twinkle

Sing and dance
now and forever
Make the sky sparkle
and your path will be bright
your steps will be illuminated

To dream is to live
To live is to dream
And if you love adventure
live by dancing
Dance here
Dance there
There is always a step
backward or forward
Dance here
Dance there
Forward or backward
You always have the choice
to start all over again

How good it is to be happy
to be a child again
full of goodness
full of kindness
with an old Soul
jumping for joy

Things of tomorrow
things of yesterday
thoughts of great longing
It is too much for my size
so I shout:
"no" to the future
"no" to the past
What is in the past, is the past
What is to come will come
whether I want it or not
but since everything here is restless
I am walking away
I am leaving with my joy
and the grapes of love in my pocket

What I want is a storm
not the storm of anger, but the storm of joy
a storm that will turn my life upside down
from the ground up

What I want is thunder
I want the thunder of love
that sweeps across the sky
of my sweet dreams

What I want is rain
rain of tenderness
that falls softly

Here I am, raising my hands in the air
like the blossom of an opening lotus
O how I long to see
what comes from above!
Arms wide open
I take a deep breath
I accept whatever comes
from the universe

Every day of the year
is spring to me
The larks' nests in my garden
Every morning
meadows of Joy
lay in my ears
melodious sounds
eternal blossom

Poetry

Poetize, my friend
on every page of your life
in every corner of the world
you are more than a writer

Travel on the roads of life
Write, write poetry
through the gardens of existence
Write, write poetry
on every side
in every corner
You are more than a writer
You are the perfect seamstress
who knows how to dress *"Desolation"*
in robes and boots of mirth

73

Be a poet
by day and night
Be a poet
in death, in life
Be a poet
in joy, in pain
Be a poet
in song and dance

74

Where ears fail
you spread smiles
where sorrow tingles
you water flowers
All with your words
O beautiful poetess
what a great finesse!

75

When all is illusion
when all is darkness
o great poet
without defeat
you are a special seed
that bears flowers and fruit
where anger has destroyed

Gita

One thought after another
all the time, all the time
What causes me stress?
Is it the light in the dying night?

Time crushes all
that falls before its feet
Nothing escapes it
Nothing resists it
neither lies nor truth
Sorrow and happiness
are forgotten in its pocket
The body so loved has withered
Only gestures of love remain in memory
and a faint smile on its lips

Down here
where pleasures are masters
and men are slaves
life is but darkness

Nothing offends me anymore
When all is said and done
every man's fate
is the same
Damned or virtuous
we all disappear one day
leaving behind
palaces and jewels
honor and falsehood
wealth and poverty

But
in the eyes of Time
dwells the most beautiful painting
none other than the face of Love
May those who gaze upon it
May they enjoy it forever!

Gold and diamonds are stones for the sun
Shiny things no longer interest me
From now on, I will do what is right:
*"Sow the seeds of love
and reap the fruits of wisdom"*

Long ago
I looked down the river of the world
and saw the devil's feint
with gold in his eyes
and silver in his smile
But here is the truth:
"When the gems are gone
the stars in the sky remain
whose brightness dances forever
in death or in life"

82

He who lives in himself
knows that we are alike
Serenity or confusion?
We make our own choices
and sometimes
we forget that only Love is king

83

Since the beginning of the world
what I have seen until now
is that phrases of Love
have conquered Time

Wisdom

85

Turn back on this road of despair
I tell you that anger is a poison
and madness
is when you hide your smile

86

If you have a thousand dreams
choose one at a time
Dreams are stars
And the good archer
does not aim at two targets

When pleasures
and desires are absent
they create suffering
When they overflow
they create boredom

In the face of death
gold has no value
Only in the Soul
lies the sacred treasure
far from the ego that burns
the walls of pleasure

Within me
everything is beautiful and flawless
There lies the void
No water, no sand, no wind, no fire
Only the endless consciousness
Like a boundless sea
Beyond day and night
Only eternity
Only ME

You who are drunk
be the trunk
of the baobab tree
when the wind of vanity
sweeps over the landscape

91

Joy is nowhere to be found
It flees from the fearful
and greedy spirit
like the deer from the panther

92

The path of serenity
is hard to find
It is one among thousands
concealed from those
who live without Love

93

All your problems
were born
in the cradle of impatience

Observe yourself in silence
Listen with your heart
and chant with the universe
The universe speaks
The universe sings
The answer to your problems
lies beside you

95

If you want a good existence
you must speak to the tortoise
which has the key to patience

Walk softly
speak softly
respond calmly
At the end of the day
lie down and sleep easy
It's a good life

*"Beware, beware
passion is a poison"*
You who desire beauty
Belladonna is on the way
Belladonna, beautiful flower
with majestic robe
and the fragrance
of enchantment
Admire it, but do not covet it
Observe it, but do not consume it
Belladonna is beautiful
But I sing and repeat
*"Beware, beware
passion is a poison"*

98

Men are straw
that cover the universe
So be patient, be kind
and remember:
*"One drop of hate
can set the world on fire"*

Before my beloved father left, he told me: *"Son, don't look at the world with your eyes. Observe it with the eyes of the sun. That is how you will know your purpose."*
"Love all things. Love all things," he murmured at the last moment.
Be at peace, father
The love you taught me
is eternal

He who comes and goes
detached from the world
has actions of gold
that do not corrode
and never fade
A thousand years hence
this soul will still be remembered

Deeds of gold build no palaces
but project many smiles
So be the wind, my friend
detached from the world
and display your pearly white teeth
Do not hide your beauty

Love yourself
love your neighbor
love the universe
and love the questioning
If you make it so
fate may deceive you
death may surprise you
but your life will not be
a flash in the sky

Go ahead
The paths are clear
and your destiny lies
neither in the past nor in the future
It is the diamond in the earring of each moment
So beautify yourself
Walk confidently
with the jewels of each moment

Do not be afraid
for no one walks alone
Everyone longs for your success
Everything is your family
Forests, stars, seas, moons, suns, deserts, and rivers
they all dance in the concert of your existence

Forget the bills that must be paid
Ignore the agonies that need to be cured
Let go of the fear that scarcity creates
Expand the heart that will soothe your face
Gratitude, gratitude
Everything is gratitude

Walk away
from the palaces
Go away
into the heart of silence
Join your hands
Radiate gratitude
The world will be grateful to you

It is a blessing to love your son
It is a blessing to love your wife
It is a blessing to love your daughter
It is a blessing to love your husband
But to love LOVE and to serve IT
is the collection of all blessings

Write the lines of your life
with the words of love
and the people who read you
can rejoice in absolute bliss
and forget their sorrows

The flowers of Life
lush or withered
speak only of beauty

Suffering and joy
are parts of life
But Love
whose understanding
is beyond all
is the ultimate way
the only road
that leads to true Life

Songs of the Soul

At the end of my past life
all forms turned to ashes
Vanity of vanities
all truth lost its meaning
I sat in the temple
where silence reigned
and I heard:
*"The whole universe is within you
and you can feel it
if you want to"*
Then I smiled and agreed
with the absolute truth

Come and dance with me
in the opera of Life
Come and dance with me
on the stage of existence
which is vast and infinite

If you do not dance today
If you do not sing today
what will you do in death?
where emptiness reigns
without a stage
without an audience

Come on
Come with me
Let me carry you along
through the Joy of the Soul
Come and trust me

Through the murmur of the wind
chant the muses of the present
In silence
I hear wonderful verses of the moment
How sweet the melodies of the Soul are!

Dreams are the flutes of the Soul
when the spirit walks softly
Sweet voice with no sound
In the depths of silence
I hear the most beautiful songs
The ultimate answer
is not elsewhere
It is right here
in the garden of silence

I was told
"Go and find your truth"
So I built a road
in the land of the Soul
and began to walk

As I make my way to the address
the mind grumbles, "It is so, it is not so"
But I walk calmly and serenely
satisfied and confident

Though the rain of disbelief
falls like stones on my head
I feel drops of water slapping
my golden and smooth skin

The sun of wrath burns hot
However, I go and give thanks
Gratitude is my protector!
Gratitude is my bow!

In the corners of my lips
reign a thousand smiles
They are arrows that I shoot
when the mind attacks me

O Kindness, my great friend
come and kill my bitterness
So, I may reach my heart
where I will be master
Of the universes

Everyone enters this world
to learn many lessons
But the true learning
lies in the closet of the Soul
O invisible wardrobe that glows
open yourself!

I am Fubbi
a poet to some people
a dreamer to others
but deep down
I am neither of the two

In my inner kingdom
lies a sublime garden
where my throne glitters

Most of the time
on the shifting sands
I am but *"thoughts"*
I let myself go
amidst the veiled souls
in this confusing world
where I climb the steps
of the unknown

In the end
I am an ordinary being
who sees, thinks and judges
But sometimes, in solitude
my dreams become poetry

Author's Instagram:
@herlicpoemas

9 786500 517019